The Parrots of Villa Gruber
Discover Lapis Lazuli

JULIAN STANNARD

salmonpoetry

Published in 2011 by
Salmon Poetry
Cliffs of Moher, County Clare, Ireland
Website: www.salmonpoetry.com
Email: info@salmonpoetry.com

ISBN 978-1-907056-74-1

COVER IMAGE: © *Ka Ho Leung* | *Dreamstime.com*
COVER DESIGN: *Siobhán Hutson*

*My tongue
clacked a few prayers.*

BASIL BUNTING

Acknowledgements

Acknowledgements are due to the editors of the following publications, in which versions of these poems have previously appeared:

TLS, The Spectator, Poetry Review, Poetry London, Ambit, Poetry Wales, Magma, South, The Red Wheelbarrow, The Interpreter's House, The SHOp, Versal (Amsterdam), *Rialto, Poetry and Audience* and *Dogs Singing: A Tribute Anthology* (Salmon).

Poems have fared well in the Poetry London Competition, The Kent and Sussex Poetry Society Open Competition, The Tunbridge Wells Competition, The Yorkshire Open Competition, and several Troubadour Poetry Competitions. 'Soup' was awarded second prize in the Strokestown International Competition 2010 and 'The Seabirds of Pimlico Hanker after Sapphires' won the Troubadour Prize in 2010.

I'd also like to thank the Bogliasco Foundation (Italy) which awarded me a Literary Fellowship in 2008. A wondrous month at the Villa dei Pini allowed me to write several of the poems which appear in this book.

This Book is for Jack and William

Contents

Zena

The Forgotten City of the South

Zena

Italia Nuda e Formicolante

I woke to find Pasolini stretched out on the bed:
his body glittering with light from the *baracce*.

When he said Italy was naked and swarming
he was taking a jewel out of the shit and they killed him.

A Sea Captain's Letter to Miss Sarah Woodruff

I'm reading Mister Fowles' account of the manner
in which you threw away your *fanciullezza*.
If I may make an observation, the only mistake I think you made
was that you opted to do this with a Frenchman.
I'm a retired sea captain from the ancient port of *Genova*.
If you wanted to pursue the game of love a little further
you could do worse than come to my city.
There are many navigators here, and the sea is in our blood.
You could live with myself and my ailing wife.
I am not rich but I am kind and I'm still quite able.
Mister Charles' advice was good: you must away from the town of *Lyme*.
I could arrange a ship's passage, good horses.
I have spoken to my wife who's very understanding.
Signorina, you are welcome here. Do not throw yourself off the cliffs.

Barbers

When I have my hair cut in the city of Genoa
the barbers are merely corpses.

They idle for days in the necropolis
and then appear in Salita Santa Caterina or Via Palestro.

They stand at the doorway, almost voluptuously:
barbers who love the dalliance of butchers.

When they push my head into a basin of water and hold it
I beat the basin with my hands

one, two, three, one, two, three, one, one,   one

The Blessing of Salami at Sant' Olcese

I'm drinking coffee at *Mangini's*,
I'm going to walk to Piazza Manin.
There's a little wind, the sky is blue.
I've seen a few pictures of paradise.

I'm taking the train to Casella,
I'll break the journey at Sant' Olcese.
The priest is blessing salami.
Anything that breathes is blessed.

Casella, Casella, Casella:
I haven't been there for twenty years
but I've been to Paraguay
or maybe a place that looks like Paraguay.

If only you could imagine Piazza Manin:
they're selling flowers and focaccia,
I'm getting high on jasmine.
If only you could imagine Piazza Manin.

Quick! Quick!:
here comes that crazy little train for Casella.
If you miss it
all the salami will have gone into the air

and the priest have nothing to bless
but a liver *malinconico*.
I haven't been to Casella for years
but I've been to Paraguay

or maybe a place that looked like Paraguay.
The train is now a mountain goat
and the seats as hard as luck.
There's a little wind, the sky is blue.

The Blessing of the Octopus at Lerici

Ever since an octopus raised itself
above the water and threw its tentacles
around the church bell and heaved it
this way and that way in order to tell us
the corsairs were coming to plunder
we have continued to bless the octopus.

That hasn't stopped us from eating it.
After all eating is a kind of blessing
and the priest who hasn't quite managed
to get the sand out of his shoes and
who comes from good peasant stock
throws on a green-braided jacket
and treks down to the gathered boats.

In truth he'd rather be tucking into
a plate of clams or a magnificent chop
than fooling around with an octopus
but he's got his psalter and he's learnt
a few lines from the poet Sbarbaro.

Water's sprinkled and there are chants
and the octopus raises itself from
under the sea and wraps its tentacles
around the poet-priest and pulls him
down to the weeds where psalters slip
and jackets bloom. There's sunlight
on the surface of the water: the priest
is cuttlefish and the priest is bone.

Bar Degli Specchi

What I want now is a little Vivaldi
which is terribly *infra dig* in some quarters
but sitting here in The Bar Of Mirrors
where I have been sitting for twenty-five years
drinking a pale version of Green Tea
which is delicately fused with ceramic blue
a Vivaldian quick step might do the trick.
It would be so much better than the song
which is coming from the radio which has something
to do with a bell and the exhortation
to ring it and to ring it and failing that
to lie prostrate on the floor and simply shudder.
If Vivaldi is no longer available or too *infra dig*
a little slow jazz or even a little low jazz
would capture the mood of the city
not to mention the mood of this Green-Blue Tea
which is holding up the sweetness of my tart.
And whilst I have been talking to you
distracting you from the drumbeat of the heart
so many things have been happening:
the mirrors are gleaming and the girl with the cloth
has created a new world order
and the boy, quite beautiful, with his *cioccolata calda*
is lowering a brioche into the dark soup…

Plan B

We're trundling down Via Balbi
past palaces of glory and endless virtue.

We're fecund with children, we're good at that
and some of us have rabbits in our pockets.

We are fluent in sundry dialects
and we're going down to Caricamento

to board a steamer for America.
The crossing will not be comfortable.

We'll be sleeping cheek by jowl, cheek to cheek
the air so foetid.

When we arrive at Ellis Island
some of us will be examined for lunacy.

How many legs does a dog have?
Who is the President of the United States?

Ligurian Paradise

Don't worry, I'm not going to talk about rocks
and I'm not going to talk about those pine trees
throwing their shadows across the garden
of the villa where – bizarrely – I'm now lodged.
And certainly no mention of Il Monte di Portofino
thrusting its leonine snout into the Ligurian waters.

And why should I talk about olives
when I crush them underfoot on my perambulations?
I'm not going to refer to the *spiaggia libera*
when here everything is free and where the women
of the market are drowning slowly in perpetual spring
coming up for air in bucolic kitchens.

Nor am I going to talk about that funicular of poets
who are glazing the surface of Genoa wishing
they had remembered pencils and scraps of paper.
And why should I waste my breath on the whirlpools
of Bogliasco or the spine of that boy which runs down
his back like a reef of surprises?

I refuse absolutely to talk about *le clair de lune*
which breaks across the sea and taps upon my window
oh so lightly and you won't believe me when I tell
you about the octopus which climbed into the villa
and wrapped its tentacles around my liver and
hoisted it up as if it were a busted cuttlefish.

And cats! I will not regale you with stories about
gatti which sometimes take on the form of *topi*
slipping insouciantly into *caruggi* and waiting for
a songwriter to find them a house that overlooks
the sea and I suppose it'd be almost churlish
not to mention Montale – well now I have.

Will it be coffee with Eusebio in Rapallo
watching the Generals in their peculiar hats
under the olive tree? I'd rather slip into
phantasmagoric Genova with its galactic towers.
And in case you're worried that I'm feeling lonely
I'm going to talk about the enchanting Suki.

The Parrots of Villa Gruber Discover Lapis Lazuli

We had spent so much time thinking about just this moment
that we took on a flat at the very top of a very tall building

which had a stairway that led you to a precarious look-out.
The views of the sea! Some days I thought I had turned into Zeus.

We rented the flat, a flat which was quite impractical, because
its corridors led into rooms and out again into yet more corridors,

the floors were wooden and the ceilings almost as high as cupolas.
When the sun shone, which was often, we were drenched in light

and sometimes the most unlikely parrots landed on the window sills.
I even wondered if it might be wrong to live in such a dazzling world!

And we came across this idea that you might live without the usual things
which meant that we were drunk on space and crazed visions.

Sometimes I came home with a bottle of Dolcetto
and we sent the children away to a friend who was always kind to them

and we looked at each other and thought Yes, it could happen soon.
And then it did. I can't recall exactly what the music was

but it was a music that allowed us to take off our shoes and our stockings
and dance and dance and dance down this corridor and through that room

and down yet more corridors and along exquisite, derelict floors.
It is this, years later, even though you would have given Pontius Pilate himself

a run for his money and even though, and how I shrank at the thought,
you dragged my name this way and that way through the Palace of Justice

and even though you built a moat around everything I had come to love –
the things I could tell you about those journeys in the dark,
     hand on the tiller!

the parrots in their colourless sleep in the careless gardens of the Villa –
it is this I remember and sometimes I think of taking out a glass
     and raising it to you.

Ciao Capo

Don't ask me if they're fake
and don't say, Will you be here tomorrow?
because I might be dead tomorrow
and how very silly to imagine
that I would have a shirt which fits.
You look bad in it Mister because you're fat.
Try not eating for a week or so,
try living in Senegal for a year or two.
Try saying *Ciao capo, ciao capo, ciao capo*.
Try saying I'll have some towels next time
what colour do you like?
Try carrying these bags along the beach all day
then try doing it tomorrow and the day after.
Try pulling out a shirt and holding it there
and try looking at a stiff white finger
which says *non non* like some crazy windscreen-wiper.
Try folding the shirt up neatly
and putting it back into the bag
and then lifting the big bags and the little bags
onto your shoulders and then going down
for the bags which have not yet been lifted
I tell you Mister time whizzes by!
Who gives a fuck about Fred Perry-Perry?
Just put your hands into your wallet
and give me twenty euros or thirty euros
or better still run to the bank machine
and get out every euro you can
then stuff them into my pockets.

Bruno Cuts My Hair in
a Place Called Ether

Never to walk in Piazza Marsala
or cut through the Mercato Orientale
buying *filetti* for his grandson Jack.
Never to make a dish out of zucchini flowers.
Never to walk down Salita Santa Caterina
or pass through the Galleria Mazzini.
Never to stand on the quayside of Genoa
with a suitcase full of straps and strings.
Never to take out a map of the world and say
I was there and there and there and there.
Never to tell the joke about the hot lemons.
Never to walk to Lavalu and see the dead
or participate in the great Ligurian lamentation
which is lupine recreation and catharsis.
Never to walk in The Street Of Perfect Love
or rub Rina's back under dim-lit chandeliers.
Never to open the fridge and find a robin.
Never to hear the sirens, never to cook a rabbit.
Never to curse God, *Porco Dio! Porco Dio!*
Shave me Bruno, caress me with scissors.
Magnificent masseur, pull out thy electric hand!

My Beautiful Son Cooks Me An Octopus

by hiring a boat in the fishing village of Camogli and heading off
for the waters of Zoagli. He has his hand firmly on the tiller
and he's telling me that one day he's going to be a champion boxer.

He's taking me to Zoagli because he wants me to see the fish.
I don't tell him that when he was born the fish leapt clean out of the se
nor do I tell him that when his mother was going crazy

the fish of Zoagli flew straight into my head and flapped.
I don't say, Son if you could open my head and let the fish go free
I might take the day off and pretend that life was sweet.

Bringing Mussolini Back to England

I flew into Rome to collect my liturgical vestments
and pick up a knocked-down Padre Pio in the New Year Sales
but I got side-tracked in *Via Del Clementino*
and chanced upon the head of Mussolini.
They wanted three thousand euros for the *Duce*
but – hah! – I beat them down, I beat them down!

Rome

You didn't tell me
you lived in the far-flung *banlieux* of the city.

I catch a train, a tram, a bus
and walk through poppies and scrubland,

I even pass the city of soldiers.
I think I've forgotten everything.

Then I wake and it all makes sense:
I'm in a vertical Corbusier world

dotted with birds
and you're standing there in a kimono!

Aubade

'Enzo smoked seven cigarettes in 60 minutes
and smiled a broken-toothed, methadone smile.

I burbled at the largeness of his back
and when I touched him he came so quietly.

It was around 5 am when he fell asleep.
Genova La Superba bleached in *Alba*:

my little swallows were going crazy in the sky.
When he slept his face thickened

into the last throes of the Republic of Salò.
It was as if I'd bedded Mussolini.

DOLCE E DECORUM EST PRO PATRIA MORI.
How sweet it is to sleep with the enemy!'

Villa Giovanna

Welcome to the Sailors Chapel and Reading Room
where there's an array of bibles
& evangelical currents are blowing down the corridor.
We could talk about the spirituality of seafaring
or we could lie down and sleep, our beds now still.
When I wake I'll put on those red slacks
& walk to Principe and then onto Via Balbi
where I'm sure to meet Signora Balbi:
Salve Signora Balbi, salve! Salve Giulio!
I'll step into the Faculty of Foreign Literature
& walk up to the loggia which is holding off the sun:
I'm going to talk at length with *carissimo* Sertoli
because he's turning into Marcello Mastroianni.
Look, he's getting out those lethal cigarettes.
But I've not smokèd for two whole years!, he says
(now rather sadly putting them away). He pats my arm:
Giulio, I have a strategy & he takes out an elegant stick
of liquorice & begins to chew & he takes out another
which he hands to me and says, It's not so bad, is it?
not — mind you — as good as the camel
but something nevertheless to put into the mouth.
We are chewing liquorice on the loggia
casting into the past, our cloud of disbelief
& now when there's a hiatus in our liquorice talk
I notice a shadow throwing itself across the loggia
& see the illustrious Bacigalupo striding forwards,
an expert on Wallace Stevens, he too is wearing slacks!
Liquorice and comity. Elegance and intelligence.
Ho preso due piccioni con una fava!
I continue past the Church of Annunziata
next to the Liceo Classico where my son learnt Latin
but stumbled over Greek. And Via Lomellini, Via San Luca,
Piazza Banchi, Piazza Campetto (ah the shop that made
my wedding rings…) & the church of San Matteo,

church of christenings & *bonbonniere*.
The old lean priest is standing in the piazza.
Sin is beautiful, he says, sin has many gaudy wings
& without it I would be out of a job and he winks
placing a hand on my shoulder and pointing up
to The Miracle of the Ethiopian Dragons by Luca Cambiaso.
I push up through the Salita Archivescavato
Migone the wine shop is there on the corner!
& onto the Questura in Piazza San Matteotti.
City of sweat and city of debt.
I'm looking at the left flank of the Doge's Palace
the white hips of the Doge's Palace
& I'm climbing the stairwell of denouncements
to greet the carabiniero who arrested me
for crimes in Villa Gruber.
It's hot now – *caldo, caldo, caldissimo*.
See how the sweat leaps from one onto the other
see how the ragazzi are wearing their *occhiali scuri*
the swinging cocks of the *vicoli*:
the Duomo and Via San Lorenzo. Left Bank of the city:
Via Fava Greca, Piazza Sarzano. Oil tankers,
Salita Fava Greca, kiff and *marocchini*:
my back to the tower, eyes seawards like Poisedon
why not ascend to San Nicolò, the quickened air beyond?
I take the funicular to Via Preve
& walk to Villa Giovanna.
I'm in the shower, the blue-tiled shower room
I'm scrubbing the sweat off myself
Oh listen! My liver's playing a little tune
& there's a white towel, almost a beatitude
& the city's turning into Havana with Scottish castles
& Ruth's on the terrace holding a melon
I've never seen such a voluptuous thing!
Come, eat, she says, I have cooked.

My Son Jack Drives his Boat to Nervi

and back. The sea is chopping up
and Filippo his mate lights up a joint
and on a day like this such clarity!

It's a wonderful thing to splice the waves
looking for oil-slicks and the dispossessed:
just a *rapidissimo* call to the guards

and everything seems to be adding up.
I like to think of Captain Jack
driving his boat to Nervi then back.

I like to think of the water's bounce.
I like to think of beauteous fish.
I like to think of the journey back.

What Did I Find On Bogliasco Beach

Bottle-tops, bottle-tops, bottle-tops
grey stones and some smaller red ones too

desiccated seaweed, *stuff mostly* and
something that had once hung from a tree.

And oh yes I found a pair of lips.

Furthest, Fairest Things

Darkness has fallen
upon the Ligurian hills
and a warm breeze
blows across the terrace.

My hosts' hormonal daughters
take another shower
and we are gazing at the stars.

That, says Marco, is a mozzarella
and he's right:
the sky is full of them tonight.

Boccaccio speaks of this
and Chaucer makes recondite
allusions in the *Astrolabe*.

Look, says Marco, see how close it is!
We hold our breath
and watch the lovely thing
shoot low across the valley.

Later a mozzarella on our plates
daughters dressed and sweetly scented
we toast the mysteries of the sky.

Oliver

I'm in Lorsica
and there's not a cigarette in sight.

But there's Oliver:
the most *simpatico* mongrel in Liguria.

He's small, he's whitish:
his eyes are popping out of his head.

I wish I could smoke him.

High Tide

How delightful to be a Julipet model
lodged in the window of an Italian boutique.
The one I'm looking at is fully clothed
and his *pièce de résistance* is a brown jumper
but why not have a look at those eyes.

He seems to have moved into underwear.
He's wearing a vest and a pair of pants
and holding his chin as if he were imitating
a man who has to make a decision
that will be of no importance whatsoever.

See how his nipples are branching out!
Imagine wearing such underwear forever
never having to take it off or put it on
and never assailed by a terrible thought.
But he has been extraordinarily busy:

for here he is in a suit and a tie and he seems
to have rustled up a rather nice briefcase.
I feel that I ought to give him a name
now that we've seen how bold and
bashful he can be. A little later I catch a train

which takes me along the coast to a city
and, look, Cosimo's ventured into cosmetics!
He's thrown off his suit, his tie and vest
and chosen a pair of astringent pants
which is just what you need on a day like this

when you're glistening with *Eau Sauvage*.

Late Swimming

When I want to be near my brother
I walk into the sea and swim breaststroke
so that my chest and stomach are
pointing down and I can feel his finger

scraping its way down my front which is
peculiar but homely too, and when
I've swum a sizeable distance
I tread water which feels like I'm sitting

on his shoulders which is wonderful
and then I know I must head back
because the boats are becoming
an archipelago of lights calling

the fish into their nets, the very fish
that will beat a little jig
on the market slabs when
the city's clattering into life.

But my brother always holds my feet
and I can see the shore slipping
into the cocktail hour and I have
to speak to him, but not unkindly.

Brother, it's so good being with you
and I'm glad you're doing well
but my time has not yet come
and people are waiting on the shore

and I feel his hands let go
which means I can really strike out now
and soon the shore is coming fast
and this time I don't look back.

Oh, Fuck It

You're dawdling on a hammock and somehow out of nowhere
you spot that crouching tiger
glittering from deep within the horizon's schizophrenic eyeball.

You climb out of the hammock
because you've not yet changed into Dalí's Son of God.
Almost four legs
you're hurtling through those dunes like a napalm dog.

Wondrous songs are slipping into the sea like turtles
and you've hauled yourself onto some great melancholic throb
because you somehow knew it was the moment of the *Diva*.

You're going to hang around forever in the asylum of the whitebait.
The sea will crack with electrifying voices.

The Seedy School of English

If I were to set up a school
I'd call it The Seedy School of English.
It'd be in some unremarkable Italian town
which already had The Oxford School
of English, The Regent School of English
even The Shining School of English.

One shows a man with a bowler hat
and a caption – mistranslated perhaps –
A Hard Teacher is Good To Find.
Another shows a protruding tongue
emblazoned with the Union Jack.
Another reveals an emblematic oyster.
I'd put up a flickering neon light.

I can tell you The Seedy School of English
wouldn't be very big:
maybe two rooms, or even one
and a reception area just perfect
for a girl called Rosalba.
One of the requirements of the job
would be a low level of English.

Not that Rosalba would appear very often:
partly because The Seedy School of English
wouldn't be rolling in it
and partly because of a medical condition
that would prevent her from doing anything
apart from getting pregnant.

I'd definitely put up a picture
of a London taxi and a double-decker bus
a map of the underground perhaps
and something with the Queen
and a poster which says
'When a Man is Tired of London
He is Tired of Life'.

Riviera Blues

After she'd gone absolutely
mental in the Continental
I took Gloria to the Astoria.

The Forgotten City
of the South

Heist

The plastic bag didn't just wander
into Michelle's Kitchen in a shucksy kind of way
now that Michelle had wedged the door open
to get some freshness into her establishment.
It made its entry as bombastic and determined
as a dawn raid organised by Special Forces:
it shot in like an arrow an inch above the ground
to sweep up shavings of noodle and cracker.
Michelle, who's from Hong Kong and who isn't
in truth actually called Michelle though she's
become accustomed to the whey-like softness
of that name, stooped to pick it up, she whose
hand has wrapped itself round duck and pancake.
Reversing like a kid on a council estate
the bag charged back into the street then kited
its way above the park, hooking itself onto a tree
which is the preferred place for plastic bags.
It hung there, Michelle standing in the doorway
in afternoon bemusement, with its microbes
and noodle-droppings in temporary crucifixion
like a poor, poor boy a long way from home.
Where shall I go next, it asked itself, Swindon?

Better Than Having A Crazed Man

There's a city
with its lights dimmed
laid out notionally
on the principles
of *illuminismo*
which includes
swathes of water
though possibly
this is a trompe d'oeil

Sometimes you're blessed
with the cleanliness of a vision
and we call this *the goose, the goose*

The city is proud of
its recalcitrant trams
and I've stood at almost
every vital point
moving my arms about
as if I were trying to guide
a wounded bird
to the safety of a nook
these gestures mean
little to the drivers

Which means that although the city
let's call it *Europa, Europa*
is generous with its provision
you never catch that ride
the trams may be a trompe d'oeil

the whole of Europe a trompe d'oeil

But sometimes at night
you catch a hint of the trams' poetic
which is better – surely – than having
a crazed man climbing through the window

Ah yes, our city of trams
precipitates an inevitable melancholy
and even now
I'm feeling that melancholy

Sometimes the sun appears
and that's peculiar
and sometimes someone speaks
and that's even more peculiar
a baffling conversation
of many languages
none of which makes sense
though if you listen carefully
someone will slip in a word
which sounds like *tram*
and I'm grateful for that

Big Rain

Big rain is coming over England
Big rain is sluicing the streets of Soho
Big rain is hammering the doorway in which I was quietly mugged

Big rain is drifting in and out of my pockets
a late spring cleaning, a reckoning
Big rain is falling upon St.Paul's

as it fell upon the heads of Michael and Alexander and that was seemly
even if the Canon insisted on her joke
Big rain is coming over England

Big rain is scrubbing at the stings of death
Big rain is drawing my brother's body away from the South China Sea
and hauling it up the Thames

I saw my brother's body from the Millennium Bridge
I saw him floating like a broken angel
I saw my brother re-gathered in the Thames

I Hear The Voices That Will Not Be Drowned

Miss Hambling's beach-bound scallop
has been severely pummelled by a wild storm.

Snooks, the local dog, also received a battering:
his harried barking was heard in several pubs.

Villagers of Aldeburgh were seen with ropes
but self-harm rarely entered their thoughts.

Later the storm dwindled and the sky turned pink.
Villagers took candles to their beds and read.

And the good scallop did not go back to the sea.
Snooks has cocked his snoop. Crabs sing. All is well.

Oh

Maud took a bottle of pills
swam into the sea
and waited for the elements.

She was washed up
near Melbourne but wasn't dead at all.

Aunt Lou went in for a lobotomy
but died under the anaesthetic.

Grandma at the end of her tether
put her head in a gas oven
and that went according to plan.

Which leaves Phyllis my agent
with Multiple Personality Disorder
which has its downsides
but seems to work in my favour.

Don't Die

My soul is humming along the Thames
is an ill-advised way to begin a poem
unless you're Keats or overcome by
such a Keatsian swoon
which on a day like this near Pimlico
when you're strolling by the river
offering your heart to Lambeth Palace
is not so difficult to believe.

I saw a lot of blood in the hospital.
I used to staunch the blood
and truth to say I was a specialist
when it came to blood. In fact it is
the word which rhymes most perfectly
with flood and on a day like this
near Vauxhhall I am waiting for the river's
gaudy ink to splash against the banks.

See me clutching arteries!
St Thom's, hospital of blood
I cannot recognize it but that was where
the painful contract was beaten out
which served me well and served me ill:
pulse, poetry, pulmonary visions.

My soul is humming along the Thames
and I am drifting in and out of Fanny
is an ill-advised way of continuing a poem
unless you're dying or dead or feel
a magpie standing on your heart which
on a day like this on the banks of the river
when all that's left is a summer breeze
is not so difficult to believe.

From under the surface of the Thames
the dead are blowing bubbles:
imagine phalanges of men and women and
little children all dressed in sartorial black
and so perfectly choreographed.
They want to sing but when they open
their lungs they send a great volley
of bubbles to the world which cannot see them.

A Post-Modern City In The Fog Which is Now A Modernist City And Therefore Unreal

How wonderfully mashed up and serene a fog-bound city is.
The anomie of bourgeois glitter, a metropolis of piano-tuners
now that the grand piano has turned into a coffin.
A city of fugues with Schubert's fantasy of corpses:
Ich liebe, Ich liebe the gothic spasms of the soup kitchen
whose stock is made from the bones of elegant boutiques!
The cobbled streets of immigrant quarters and Liverpool Street.
Buildings of glass like ships at sea carrying the money curse
and the helmsman lashed to the tiller, the albatross more bat than bird.
These shirts are beautifully pressed and scented
ready to wrap themselves around the torsos of the rich
but now the rich are a little less rich and the shirts
are resting under the blue light of a sleeping shop which declares
Reductions of 50% and even 80% and Buy Two Quality Shirts
and you can swagger up Brick Lane and visit the studio
of Tracey Emin who's forsaken Margate's heart-stopping beaches.
How riveting to stand on the rooftop of Das Kapital
and see the world as we've come to know it disappearing under
a whirr of blades and hysterical faces.
Someone's written KEEP WARM – BURN THE BANKERS
but I think a guillotine might be quicker.
You buy a ½ price suit and walk through the city
but the city doesn't see it because the city's only a shape in the fog,
the brothel-meat thrown out with the brothel.
Unreal city's wounded like a real dog and I follow it
down Folgate Street to *The Poet*, where we drown ourselves.

Diachronic Time

This is not diachronic time, this is pram in the garden time.
There's a rather large weeping ash out there
and it's being blown around by an August wind.
There's a pram under the tree with a white net over it
which will keep that old-fashioned baby far from harm.
The wind is blowing hard but it's a warm wind
and the baby which is sleeping, ah, what a wonderful baby!
is beginning to cry, and it's moving those little arms
and those little legs up and down and up and down.
When I next look in the pram it is completely empty
but now there's a baby in it, and now it is empty.
Baby, empty, baby, dog – I think it's a Jack Russell.

I believe we're watching cricket at the Oval.
Mr Boycott's coming in with a banana swinger
and look there's Peter May! Or is it Colin Cowdray?
I'm sitting next to my mother and she's holding
a rather large box of smoked salmon
because tomorrow my sister's going to be married.

Portrait of Isabel Rawsthorne Standing in A Street in Soho

Birth, and copulation, and death.
That's all the facts when you come to the brass tacks.
Birth, and copulation, and death

and a black forest blanched with frost
and a sheep maybe, and a walk along the street
and going to the butcher's for a chop

and coming back with *osso buco*
and a little tip-tap on the corner
if it doesn't look easy you aren't working hard enough.

And bumping into Isabel Rawsthorne
who's standing in a street in Soho
who doesn't look very well somehow

who looks as if she's lost her keys
who looks as if she's lost her foot
who looks as if her face's gone awol.

Hi Isabel, I say, I've got a bag of *osso buco*.
I wanted to buy a chop or a little bacon
but I ended up with *osso buco*.

Miss Moon

Sometimes I wake in the early hours
and worry about Miss Moon.
Letters for her are piling up in the hallway,
I think of her fingering Chicken Kiev
and abandoning the cheese cake.
I see her opening the wardrobe and thinking of a dress,
sex is not without a dose of stress.
What can a girl do with cloth so thin?
Sometimes Miss Moon runs naked from the bathroom
and sticks her head into a bag.

Sometimes I wake in the early hours
and worry about Miss Moon.
Letters for her are piling up in the hallway,
I think of her boiling a kidney
and dabbing her eyes with carpaccio.
I see her opening the wardrobe and looking for leather,
I think Miss Moon is rather clever.
What can a girl do with such a Weimar look?
Sometimes Miss Moon runs naked from the bathroom
and sticks her head into the freezer.

Sometimes I wake in the early hours
and worry about Miss Moon.
Letters for her are piling up in the hallway,
I think of her making a rabbit pie
and rubbing garlic across her tongue.
I see her opening the wardrobe and choosing a whip,
I think Miss Moon is rather hip.
What can a girl do with such libido?
Sometimes Miss Moon runs naked from the bathroom
and sticks her head into the sun.

Her Peculiar Oblations

sorted it weeks ago
so I don't have to pour oil
down my ears. I do anyway.

'Twice a day, twenty minutes'
said Nurse Florid in April
and then quite dreamily

as if considering the eye of the needle
'April *is* the cruellest month.'
Then she heaved herself

around the Treatment Room
in a miasma of giggles.
'Oh, I do love ears!'

shooting her syringe
towards the ceiling
like the cowgirl in a B-Movie

who gives it hard
and takes it hard
and who, by the end, *is just one of the boys.*

When I walked out
of Nurse Florid's Treatment Room
in dazzling April

my ears were so clean
I thought of banging out
an Alleluia with the Baptists.

I miss Nurse Florid
and her peculiar oblations.
I do it for her mostly.

Le Lion Rouge Est Sur La Table

Don't forget to say *Madame* Hoare, my mother said.
Bonjour *Madame* Hoare, I said; Bonjour Julien said *Madame* Hoare.
I really liked Madame Hoare because she had a red lion.
She said, Julien where is the red lion?
I said, Madame Hoare the red lion is on the floor.
Madame Hoare took the red lion and placed it on the table.
Julien, écoute, où est le lion rouge?
Madame Hoare, I said, le lion rouge est sur la table.
Bien sûr, le lion rouge est sur la table!
French, I decided, was a beautiful and accurate language.

Several days later I was bitten by a snake.
Madame Hoare sent a letter saying she was worried.
At the end of the letter she wrote *Julien, où est le serpent?*

Years later I found myself in Paris.
I think I'd forgotten almost everything about Madame Hoare.
She might have died.
Perhaps the snake which had nearly done for me
had wound its way out of our garden of rumbutans
and slipped across the island
with the sole purpose of biting Madame Hoare.
Où est le serpent? JE SUIS ICI!

Years later I was sitting in a café on the Left Bank.
I was talking to a Frenchman who was worried.
Julien, he said, *où est La Liberté?*

I looked across the table and saw a lion which was red
and behind the bottle of Pernod I saw a moving snake.

I said, *La Liberté est sur la table.*

The Bicycle

There's something about the bicycle
which makes you think of a shark
that's holding back on the accelerator
as if for a while the shark is doing nothing less
than enjoying its sense of sharkness.
A shark knows that it can bide its time,
it knows that it can withdraw to the horizon
and take you later like an open sandwich.

You see that the bicycle has your name on it
and the tall blond cyclist knows that you've seen it.
You might walk back to the flat in *Waalstraat*
or you might make your way to the market
where for now you can hide among the crowds.
For no particular reason you buy an orange shirt.

Now you're thinking of blood oranges
but you can't rid yourself of that schizophrenic bicycle:
and you remember something called relaxation
and you say Do you think I could pipe some of that into my head?
You're beginning to feel that the language
of the city is a peculiar conspiracy of clocks
so, nothing doing, you step into a coffee shop.

Once you could have ridden the bicycle yourself
and plotted your way through the fogs of the city
crossing the canals with the surge of a goose,
the Nureyev of a structured city! How young you were
and how beautifully and un-complicatedly stoned!

Now you're hunkered down in a room of mirrors.
There are two things invading the core of your being.
First that cow upside down on the ceiling, which is bad enough.
Secondly a shark which thinks it's a bicycle.
The bicycle is the one true invention of the Protestant God.

You wander into an Emporium and run your hand over Buddha.
You open a medicine box and breathe in the sweetness of the cedar.
You note to yourself that the medicine box has no medicine:
there's no pocket knife to slash the tyres of a dissembling bicycle
there's no spoke to slide among its Euclidian wheels.
Then you make your way to The Sugar Factory, how cool is that?

The Nightingale Sings in Bucharest

Imagine you have a whistle but no train
and you're standing on a small platform
outside Budapest and when I say Budapest
I might have been thinking of dust and
does the heart always leap in Bucharest?
When the map quivers you find yourself
within the necromantic dream of Turin.

It hardly matters because the platform
is just a functioning slab and the warmth
of the city has gone. Yet somehow
you know that out there in the night
is a train of people you could have loved.
Some were taken by the sea and some,
without concern for originality,
threw themselves from the cliff.

Out there in the darkness a train of the dead
is hurtling along in a fanfare of rectangular light.
In one of the carriages there's a samovar
and vodka's loosening up the corpses.
Neither can you see the train nor hear her
even when you strain like a dog.

But you know that the whistle's rhythm and
the whistle's blood can pull the train
out of Slovakia and out of Deutschland and
now that I've mentioned Slovakia is there a man
here who doesn't reach for a violin?
You're blowing your whistle in the night
which belongs to Europe and relentless sobbing

through which a train of the dead is hurtling
under the rule of vodka and eternal hip-sway
and the train catches the note of the whistle
like a nightingale and slips out of the place
in which it once was like the strange lips
of a bird giddy on anthracite and suction.

A whistle, a whistle, see what you have done.

Bare Back

That awfully distracting evening at Brigit's.
The garden's been untended for years
and is beginning to move into the house.
Sometimes a bird flies into the room
knocks something over and bolts back into the night.

That's nature, Brigit says, which reminds her:
it was so hot that I took off all my clothes
and got on the horse and rode bare back across the prairie.
Of course there wasn't a person in sight
and, goodness, I can remember the vibrations.

I sent a piece to *The Lady.*
It was 1963, I think. They published the whole thing
apart from the bit about the horse, which seems a shame really.
Anyway I've written a poem about it
which I'm going to read to you *terribly* slowly
and then afterwards I'm going to read it again.

Eileen Makes Me A Bacon Sandwich

by taking a cheap flight to Denmark
and creeping up surreptitiously on a wayside hog
and sweeping a kukri up into its flank
to get the beauty of it fresh.

She returns to England with a glint in her eye
only to remember she's forgotten the butter,
so she leaves the pork on the sideboard
and takes the next flight back to Denmark.

There she milks a cow in a somewhat bucolic way
remembers to grab some Danish pastries
and returns to England to assemble the parts.
I'm feeling peckish under the duvet.

Vic Makes Me Lasagna

by opening a tin of tomatoes and gathering a little sage
and then – yes – that little two-step towards the edge of holiness.
There was such *delicatezza* in those gestures
as if he'd spent his life making lasagna for minor poets.

Later we talked books: *The Devil in Love.*

It's about Naples – my Naples – and a camel which says *CHE VUOI*
in the most booming of voices. Vic did the voices.
The wine was good too. But Vic, I was on the point of drifting off.
And the figs! Which angel did you hire to bring those figs?

Mother Makes One Of Her
Sunday Curries

by establishing herself as the temporary head
of a quickly summoned expeditionary force
that is charged with the task of re-possessing India
so the stall holders of Mumbai
can bring out their best selection of spices
and for a strange and quite astonishing moment
the word Empress might flutter over their tongues.

A military success, the invasion stuns the world
and we watch Mother moving through the Sub-Continent
unable to find the right words for the neighbours
who are, in fact, Indian and who are unfailingly polite.
When Mother gives her numerous press conferences
she is draped in flowers and is wearing a mind-blowing Sari.
Even Bollywood is talking about her colonial dash.

Mother's wholesale acquisition of the spice markets
has made the Indian Stock Exchange somewhat giddy
but the *Times of India* is not totally unsympathetic
and one journalist insists on using the word *rampant*.
After a couple of weeks of considerable brouhaha
the world's media returns to earthquakes and floods.

Flags are raised, flags are lowered and there's a lovely band
and we watch mother standing on an impeccable lawn
holding a glass that's crackling with Angostura Bitters.
It's the monsoon season and a cricket pitch turns into a lake.
It's good to hear Mother in the kitchen with her syncopated pots
and the whole family tripping over each other with hunger.

Yes, lunch is going to be late but it's going to be worth it
and I'm helping to set the table and Daddy's knocking back whisky.
Then suddenly Mother comes into the room and says
'Do you remember those little fish we ate in Malaya?'
and I can smell the rest house and hear the guerrillas
whispering which meant we sometimes had to sleep with
a gun under the bed and the speed of the fan on the ceiling

was either slow or just very slow, the mosquito net such a joke.
We tell Mother nervously that *ikan bili* is terribly yesterday
and maybe this time we could all sit down to Sunday lunch
leaving the people of Malaya to savour their independence.
But we can see that she is torn between the fabulous curry
that drifts out of the kitchen and breathes over the house
and her nostalgic recollections of the thin crisp salty fish.

And before we have time to persuade her otherwise
Mother's slipping out of the door with a kukri
and calling Veronica who's been living in Chippenham
since Harry was tiresome enough to die.
They're organising a sunset and a large stiff drink
and a shake me down in the shower and a Rambutan Tree
and a veranda — yes — that sounds as perfumed as Veronica!

Pastoral

Mother's not whistling, she's blowing.

She's at the foot of the garden, blowing strong.
Heading towards the house
she's strafed by a couple of blue tits.

Now mother's in the house.
She's blowing her way round the kitchen
the provenance of the succulent pigeon.

Mother's making a soup of goodness, deep and hot.

She steps over dogs and cats
some stuffed, some unexpectedly winsome
and she blows her way into the bedroom.

She lies on her back and blows,
the ceiling hovers tantalisingly above the house.

Like a balloon the world's growing,

Acris Hiems

We're running out of wood, mother says.
The snow falls and the dogs growl
because they're slipping into a dog trance.

We're running out of wood, mother says.
The snow falls and the dogs growl
because we're slipping into a dog trance.

That night the electricity goes *pling*
and we sit around a tray of candles.
The dogs want to slip into our beds.

Then it's morning and Neville's there
with his wheelbarrow full of logs
and the dogs are going crazy because

they never liked him very much
but we say Oh Neville, Sir Neville
come into the house with your logs!

Soup

Soup will keep us afloat:
soup is our mainstay of hope.
That winter we washed in it
as well as ate it, great pots
of soup with beans and bones.
Mother, the farmer's daughter,
knew hearts were whittled
knew feet were cold.
Mother, the colonel's wife,
knew the wood-stove needed logs
that soup would shrive.
Soup is God's younger brother.
Soup is Corinthians.
Soup is patient, soup is kind:
it does not envy, it does not boast.

My mother gave me a pot of soup
made of beans and bones
that needed two strong arms
and a crack of the back
and I carried it to my sister
whose dogs think they are
wolves and although crows
cawed and deer peeked
and the storm did that
storm cometh number
we supped on soup so that
our chins were wet with it
and when the dead came by
and I can tell you there's
been no shortage in our house
they were buoyed by the soup
and there was no stinting.

Oh soup, keep us afloat.
Oh God's little brother
abide with me
in the kitchen of mother.

Scallops for Tracy

Steve's cooking scallops for Tracy.
He'll actually use a little too much cream
but the scallops won't resist too much.

Steve's cooking scallops for Tracy.
Everything bar the cooking's almost ready.
He's about to undress and step into the shower.

Tracy's slipping out of Darlington.
She doesn't know about the scallops,
she's not sure about her level of resistance.

Steve's scrubbing himself in the shower.
It's true he's put on a little weight
but who wants to sleep with a will-o'-the-wisp?

Steve's cooking scallops for Tracy,
he needs to shave and apply some *Eau Sauvage*.
A man with scallops is a man who shaves.

Tracy's driving along the motorway.
She's bought herself a nice little dress.
She's never in her life eaten a scallop.

And Then I Released it into the Wilderness

I was mildly surprised
when I received my first hamster through the post.

I'm no great lover of hamsters
but I dusted it down
fed it on whatever I had in the kitchen, not a lot actually
and then I released it into the wilderness.

Some time later I received a dog.

Though I'm no great lover of dogs
I fed it whatever I had in the kitchen, mostly hamsters
                                    and a little chicory
and then I released it into the wilderness.

A little later I received a horse.
I had to sign for that of course.
The postman was holding a whip and his boots
                            were spectacularly buffed.

Well, you might have guessed, I'm no great lover of horses.
I once ate one in a Parisian restaurant
having made them remove the hooves
                        and that tang of undergrowth.

It would have been cruel to mention this
as I pulled the horse out of its envelope
and led it away into my studio flat.

And because I believe in equity
I fed the horse on whatever I had in the kitchen,
                        namely hamsters, a dog
and a small tin of curry powder.

And then I released it into the wilderness.

Sardines Hit Back

It was sickening being so low down in the food chain
with practically the whole sublunary world waiting for us
to make our suicidal run, like some revolving sushi table.
Only we weren't sushi, we were sardines
swarming antipasti on a heaving holocaustic bed of ocean.
How we glittered like starlight. Eat us! Eat us!

Our tactics were sub-Ghandi: not passive resistance, just passive.
Somebody had come up with the big ball notion
making us into a collective high on the proximity of ourselves.
Who would be a single discrete sardine
when you could turn yourself into a gigantic fish fest?
We continued to murmur our one instruction *Eat us!*

I couldn't bear it anymore, lodged in the ghetto of despair
the gannets swooping in like Messerschmitts.
I was reading Jean Paul Sartre before he'd thought of nausea
and when Churchill said 'We will never surrender' I went loopy.
It was time for hit and run, pay back and commando training.
It was time to set up sardine hit squads.

Most of the guys said *Get real, we're out on a limb*
but I gnawed at their sense of vanity and found insomniacs
whose broken dreams always involved something called a tin
and when the dolphin, our smiling Jesuit, entered the congregation
I swam into the moonlight and exploded with mackerel visions.
When I got back to the throng I was lit up with charisma.

The commissar black-tipped shark ate several thousand stragglers
but I knew our evolutionary leap would have its blood price.
When one lone gannet swooped like a banshee I flinched and smirked,
I gave the nod to Stalin's men and when the gannets cut into the ocean
the sardine ballet shimmied sideways and the sharks crunched beaks.
Gannets, gannets everywhere and each one of them was wrecked!

Now that the shark and the dolphin had a taste for the seabird
we could concentrate on synchronised swimming.
Most of my people were just happy they could live a little longer,
some of the Buddhists started praying for the plunging gannet.
But I had plans for our stateless nation, we hapless Kurds of the sea.
I wanted to take the fight from under the lid of the ocean.

So I created the Sardine Liberation Organization
and set the dolphin against the shark.
We cultivated a taste for flight and established mobile flying units.
It took a lot of practice, sweat, no small amount of luck.
But we broke through the spume and took to the wing
and became the avenging gangsters of the crushed.

William's Head

William's head comes to me like a gift.
I hold it then cup it like a jewel, an egg
for what is more wonderful than a child's head?
It was the first thing I saw of him
and he had hair, goodness how much hair!

I was the first to see the head
breaking into the world like René Descartes!
It was the child's calling card, the handshake.
His mother was letting out her lupine howls.

What is more wonderful than a child's head?
An egg of love, an egg of worry.
I was only a fragment, a seed-giver.
I seem to remember I was a woodcutter.

William's head has come to me like a gift.
I will cradle it and hold it
and sear my fingers on the voltage
because a gift is a box of grief.
I reckon Lord Tristan dreamt up the whole idea.

William's head is away now.
I see it crossing land and sea
I see it crossing mountains
I hear the guns and the dogs.

Cosimo's Gift

1

Cosimo's given another bulk-buy book of photographs
full of orange crevices and weird geological formations
and thinks This is my gift to England.
He likes to say he's got a friend in what he calls Titanic City.
Most people think That doesn't sound so good
and when no-one's looking they give their testicles a pat.
All those orange crevices and crazy rock formations.
Is Cosimo hinting at suicide?

Cosimo gets another bulk-buy book of glossy photographs.
He walks to the Post Office in Kroton
and says, I'm sending this to my friend in Southampton.
The woman who handles packages nods – *Molto bene*.
It's a heavy book and the postage comes to thirteen euros.
The woman glances at Cosimo's groin.
Eventually the book leaves that forgotten city of the south
and fetches up, almost mystically, in another.

The book's now at the sorting office in Shirley.
Without reason a postman picks it up and chucks it to a mate
who chucks it to another who shimmies and sells a dummy
and breaches the Welsh defence to score a useful try.
Cosimo's book of geological weirdness is already a success.
The fever of the moment over, it's placed back in the basket
of Urgent Deliveries where it sinks down to the bottom.

A few days later the package is prepared for the outside world.
A corner of the book has punctured the yellow envelope.
A postman puts it into a red bag and climbs onto a bicycle.
A cobweb of grey is folding over the city, the postman's whistling.
He slips past the Pig N' Whistle and coasts down Landguard Road.
An inchoate melancholy drifts out of the Bail Hostel.
It's now twelve thirty, the perfect time to deliver a parcel.
The parcel too wide for the letter box, he rings the bell.

And being a postman he rings twice:
still no answer so he places his ear against the glass
and listens rapturously to the gift of silence.
Ah well, he says, back to the farm my rooster
and he pats Cosimo's book before lobbing it into his bag.
Cobweb of grey's folding over the city, postman's whistling.
He slips past the Pig N'Whistle and back to Shirley.
Melancholy winks at the Monkey Puzzle Tree.

2

I sit on the sofa and thank God for England
I sleep and wake and work I sleep I work I work I wake.
I seem to be walking along the Rio Grande.
Weeks pass. I ring in sick and that's because I *am* sick.
As Marlow was sucked into his quest for Kurtz
I begin my journey down Shirley High Street.
The *tat, tat, tat*'s turning into a burst of gunfire.
The church of Saint Boniface takes no prisoners.

Cosimo's book of monstrosities isn't in my thoughts.
This type of communication comes from a wife or a lawyer.
If it's the lawyer I'm addressed as Egregious Doctor
and invited to present myself in a foreign court
to answer charges of a vaguely nuptial nature.
If it's a wife she writes in the style of a ransom note:
a weird macaronic display of languages and letters
whose refrain is constant *Sei Un Pezzo Di Merda*.

A light wind's rattling my bones and tossing my hair.
The temptations of the Polish shop are resistible.
Will I get the Bourbon lily?
Twelve-thirty at the sorting office: my life has bobbed,
my life has bobbed, I've lit my candle for Lycidas.
I'm in the queue for minor prophets
and my passport photo suggests The Red Brigade.
The postman sighs *Cosimo!, Oh Cosimo!*

When I see the package he crashes into reality.
I should've realised my collection of photographic books
was inadequate, that the wonders of the rock are infinite:
Wonders of the New World, Wonders of Our Planet
Wonders of the Appalachians, Wonders of the Gannet.
Whatever the focus of the wonder there's a vast canyon
and a subliminal message, Don't jump, don't jump, Ok, just do it!

I could buy some synthetic hair, I could visit the pornographer.
The temptations of the Polish shop are resistible.
Cosimo's book's my shield, my root, my sticking place.
I've been spared the obiter dicta of a crazed wife.
It's still a while before I reach the outer hub of decency
so I walk with Cosimo into the Forest of Calabria.
He's brought a tripod, several meatballs, a bottle of carrot juice.
He has an astonishing vocabulary when it comes to trees.

After meatballs and a morning of tree talk
I'm rather hoping a lone wolf might slink into the frame
partly because it would be more interesting than a tree
and partly because it might bite Cosimo in the foot.
When we're not talking about trees we're talking about fish
and when we're not talking about fish we're talking about
LA VIA DOLOROSA. Cosimo's crackling with *Weltschmerz*.
He's thinking of building a hut in the forest and living in it.

Oh Cosimo, what did you do yesterday? *I cookèd fish.*
Oh Cosimo what have you done today? *I cookèd fish.*
Oh Cosimo what will you do tomorrow? *I cookèd fish.*
Oh Cosimo, Cosimo, what will you ever do, ever do?
Fish, fish, fish. Have you never seen La Dolce Vita?
And the photographs, when will you take the photographs?

When I'm not cooking all the fish, I suppose.
It's easier to die than to remember but I am remembering.
He's got a car, we're in it, driving past the Temple of Hera.
There's the light of the moon in the swoon of the waves.
If we travel further we'll reach the city of Sybarus.
The afternoon is upon me but there's no evidence of heat.
Aargh, I think there's an arrow sticking in my head.
When I get back to the flat I rip open the package.

It's not orange or brown or red, it's blue.
It says *To my dearest friend, a hug of joy!*
If you love the sea, you'll love this book.

Polski

My mother took me to the window
and showed me a dark skyline of flying horses.
Then she whispered as if in a dream, The Poles are coming.

They're galloping out of Warsaw, Krakow, Gdansk,
they've battered down the walls of the Ghetto
they're riding such ungainly little horses
but they're riding them with such panache!
Ah, just look at the cut of their gloves...

A cavalry of fruit-pickers and pie-makers.

They're cutting through the soft belly of Belgium
two fingers up to the Maginot line!
They're heading straight for Dunkirk.
Europe can only watch and tremble.

My mother who's dabbled in Walter de la Mare
and so knows about history said:
Of course they want England in general
but most of all they want Bournemouth.

When they get to the English Channel
the new whale road of the Polski
their horses grow wings and they fly
a squadron of educated Icaruses,
suitcases pullulating with meat.

I was so excited to be living in the moment
that I climbed up a rickety ladder to take in the view.
Don't fall off, my mother said
I don't think I will be able to help you.

Well-Regulated Dumplings Are Going Upwards

They're playing jazz in the Platz
which is cool because when you smile
the whole world wants a little Schnitzel.

They might be old and melancholic
but they're playing jazz in the Platz
which is cool because when you smile
the whole world wants a little Kunst.

They're playing jazz in the Platz
which is cool because they're making
little rooms in your head which
are so light and so free

that Ludwig One and Ludwig Two are going into the air
that The Rathaus mit Glockenspiel are going into the air

that the Blumen and Schweinenacken are going into the air
that there's been a sighting of Max Beckmann up in the air

that the Englisher Garten are absolutely gorgeous in the air
that Rudolf Steiner has become a special rocket

that well-regulated dumplings are going upwards
that buckets of whipped cream are going, going into the air.

This is a lightness which is lighter than light
this is a lightness which is lighter than skin
that I have to ask myself, Can this be death?
but why wrap yourself up in knots about a thing like that
because when you smile − ja − because
when you smile the whole world smiles with you.

Vonnegut's Dresden

The first fancy city I'd ever seen —
a city full of zoos and statues.
We were living in a slaughterhouse,
a nice new cement-block hog barn.

Mornings we worked in a malt syrup factory.
The syrup was for pregnant women.
The damned sirens would go off
and we'd hear some city getting it bad
whump whump whump whump.

We thought we were safe.
There weren't any shelters in our town,
just clarinet factories.
Then the sirens went; February 13th, 1945.

We went down two stories
below the pavement into a big meat locker.
It was cool there,
all those cadavers hanging around.
When we came up the city was gone.

Waiting for the Barbarians

Darling, just think
we've almost got the city to ourselves.
True, a few shopkeepers
are stocking up on cabbage
and there's a run on Schiller in the bookshop.
And yesterday at dusk
I wandered down to the river
and heard the soulful moping of a cello.

And darling, I've booked a table
at that little restaurant you've always fancied.
The menu isn't quite holding up
but they're getting in a brace of rabbits
and a bottle of wine that's almost decent.

And that dress you're wearing
I want you to take it off
and I want you to wear it forever.

Dog Talk

Why be adrift
when you could be a dog?

Why be a heaving breast
when you could be a dog?

Why take on a mortgage
when you could be a dog?

Why take a trip to Nam
when you could be a dog?

Why be an Oxford Blue
when you could be a dog?

Why be a blue stocking
when you could be a dog?

Why drool over a mozzarella
when you could be a dog?

Why stake your reputation
when you could be a dog?

Why do a Ph.D
when you could be a dog?

Why pen a sonnet
when you could be a dog?

Why broker peace in the Middle East
when you could be a dog?

Why be a lunatic
when you could be a dog?

Why be twenty-third in line to the throne
and why be Home Secretary

and why be a triple jumper
when you could be a dog?

Why be a crock of shite
when you could be a dog?

Why go to the trouble of preparing a bong
when you could be a dog?

Why be the morning mist
when you could be a dog?

Why have two legs
when you could have four or even three?

Why be a dog in the manger
when you could be the dog?

Do You Have to Live in Paris to be a Flâneur?

I'm walking down Shirley High Street.
Could someone come and get me now?

Jerry Hall Stands In For Tracey Emin

Tracey's gone away to do what she's so good at
and she's asked me to fill in for her. I'm a little nervous.

I spent so many years hooked up with Mick
that people might think I'm an intellectual – hey!

Sometimes I write poems, but not when I'm happy.
When Tracey asked me to take over the column

sure I was happy *and* nervous, but mostly happy.
Next week I'm doing the Arvon Writing Course.

Hugo Williams is my teacher. I've read his book *Dear Room*.
Hugo makes me happy and I'm nervous about that

because I just can't write poems when I'm happy.

Death of the Critic

Claude jumps down from the laundry van
parked up on the pavement in Rue Pergolèse.
He's writing a novel but he drives a van.
He lives off Boulevard Saint-Michel.
The novel isn't great but it's clever
and if there was a choice between driving a van
or signing books on the Rive Gauche
then Claude who's studied at the Sorbonne
wouldn't mind ditching the van
even if the job impresses his more radical friends
and these days his friends seem a lot more radical.
Claude banters with the boss and smokes a gauloise
and fetches over some beautiful shirts.
It's spring and he's writing a novel
and some of the smoke from the gauloise
is seeping into the shirts and that's as it should be:
it's 1968 and the world's changing.

Roland Barthes has just given a lecture
at the École Practique des Hautes Études
and although no one has understood it
there's a spontaneous outbreak of applause.
Roland Barthes, they feel, is on their side
and everyone's bored with André Gide.
Roland Barthes who's heady with adrenalin
is now stepping into Rue de Lille
and fails to notice *absolument*
the laundry van which is fast approaching.
Claude swerves and Barthes walks on.

1968's cutting into 1980.
Roland Barthes is a name to reckon with
and he teaches at the Collège de France.
And imagine this: Francois Mitterrand

who's about to become the President
invites the critic for a dazzling lunch.
Barthes is drinking champagne
but he's thinking of his mother
who's on the *Boulevard des Morts*
He says (in French) 'I can do no more
than await my total undialectical death.'
The almost President nods. Champagne?

Claude never published anything
but he's done well at the laundry:
he seems to have a knack for it.
Sometime around 1973
he read 'Death of the Author' and wept.
He only drives a van when there's an emergency
when someone's ill, now that he's the boss
but he likes being on the streets
a van full of unwashed clothes.
He's happy because his head's
buzzing with the fragments of a novel.
He doesn't see Roland Barthes
whose mother's dead, whose loves
are shadows in the boulevards
who's stepping into Rue des Écoles.

And Heaven Knows I Am Fifty Now

We were charmed when you waved your arms
above your head and clutched your gladioli
and it would be great if you took me out tonight
because when I'm riding in your car
I never want to go home, not even for a while.
And thank God you stayed clear of that bus
because if you'd been killed we wouldn't
be putting candles on your birthday cake
and now we want you to blow them out
if only to see what happens next.

You handsome devil, you charming man.
A boy in the bush is worth two in the hand
but I'm a girl and you're a boy
or was it the other way round, I don't know,
and does the body rule the mind
or does the mind rule the body, I don't know.
Shyness is nice but it definitely gets in the way.
I had this friend who didn't care for gladioli
and I can't remember if he liked
your music that much and when I put my hands
on his memory glands he just couldn't relax.

Your cake is lovely and full of lights
and although they're flickering
they don't seem to be going out.

Valleys Breathe, Heaven & Earth Move Together

After three weeks of continuous grading
I couldn't stop myself from making comments
and giving out carefully weighted scores.
So after reading 'Wales Visitation' this is what I wrote:
Allen, impressed by your energy and drive:
no shortage of rhetorical bravura
though rather promiscuous with the apostrophe,
and frankly the last time I visited Wales
it was so wet that getting on my knees
would in all likelihood have given me the flu:
'O, Great Wetness, O Mother!'
And may I suggest that future hikes in the country
would be easier if you trimmed your beard
or – maybe – removed it altogether:
'I lay down mixing my beard with the wet hair
of the mountainside/ smelling the vagina-moist ground.'
At such moments you might have considered
easing your foot *off* the accelerator.
but the project to move heaven and earth together
was, nevertheless, commendable. Ginsberg: 69

The Seabirds of Pimlico Hanker after Sapphires

I had a crazy idea we could have a good time
so you're flying in from Italy on Alitalia
and I'm booking a room in Edward Lear's old house
all sorted by my promiscuous credit card.
Then I take you to the Gay Hussar in Greek Street
where you can say anything you like
and because we're having a good time
I smile and offer you some Schnitzel.
Later, after I've paid the bill without flinching
we take a taxi to a discreet point on the Thames
where a boat is waiting full of elegant people.

It's a beautiful, limpid night and the orchestra
seems Welsh somehow. They're playing jazz but
they also throw in several Lieder. Everyone looks
good and so do you and apparently I do too
and before you know it we're dancing on the deck
a little Cole Porter and some Bunky Green
and our luminous children are following the boat
like mermaids but in actual fact they're boys
with your looks and my intelligence but
I close my mouth because the captain of the boat

deserves to live, the glittering orchestra deserves to live
and our earthly boys are hauling themselves
onto the deck as if they were part of an advert
and they see their parents dancing cheek to cheek
and before you know it we're sitting round a table
and the waiter's bringing audacious cocktails.
It feels so good it feels like cocaine but it isn't.
It feels as if all the Carabinieri and all the lawyers
have turned into seabirds flying off to Pimlico
and although it would be crazy to talk of love
the whole of London's lit up like a beating heart.

The Middle Classes No Longer Defer Their Gratifications

Goodness, I'm lying in bed listening to *The Archers*.
Sophie – or is it Marlene Dietrich? – is sweet talking David
   on the telephone.

Ruth is rushing over to the paddocks to shag Sam.
Kirsty is dressed as a dwarf and is sighing into her soup

and Linda is surfing the net for cut-price jiggle balls.
In The Bull there's talk of fixing up a sauna for gay farmers.

Ah Sunday, Sunday, that God-filled moment of rest and gratitude.

Well, Well, Well

Why don't we play that game
where you're free
to speed around the world
at the drop of a hat?

You say to me:
Come to New York on Saturday
and we'll do some shopping
in 34th Street and I say,

looking both vague and intense,
Oh but I can't, I'll be in Berlin
conducting the Philharmonic
then doing something slightly weird

in the Kurfürstendamm.
Oh well, not to worry, you say
why not do Vancouver at the end of the month:
I'm organizing a party

and Grace Jones is coming.
Oh, you devil, I say
you know I'm taking up that Fellowship
at the American Academy

in Rome
where in all likelihood I'll be interviewing
Gore Vidal.
Well, well, well, you say

and as you're saying it
there's that little jangle
you sometimes get
at the centre of the brain

and I find myself walking
slowly to the Co-op
to buy beetroot
and cigarettes.

England

England is now called Eat As Much As You Like.
Since the Beatles produced their first LP

England's hotter by a whole degree.
Olives, damn it, have been glimpsed in Dorset!

England, England, you'd be crazy *not* to live there.